T   LE BOOK OF
PROCRASTINATION

Andrea Perry

Worth Publishing

www.worthpublishing.com

First published by Worth Publishing Ltd 2003
www.worthpublishing.com

ISBN 1903269067
© Andrea Perry 2003
Cartoons by Joel Mischon © Worth Publishing

Cover and text design by Caroline Harper

Printed and bound in Great Britain by William Clowes, Suffolk, UK

For Champagne Jenny (MA),
with love

ACKNOWLEDGEMENTS

To all the people who have shared their experiences of procrastination with me in therapy and workshops: to everyone who gave me feedback on *Isn't It About Time?* and encouraged me to write more: to my supportive friends and family, Jenny, Catherine, Bruce, Louize, Ian, Petra, Liz, Jonbon, Cara, and to Ursula for her love: to Kyla and Marie-Carmen at Worth Publishing for their consistent hard work and good humour: to Caroline the designer, who is such a pleasure to work with: and especially, as ever, to Martin – to all, my thanks.

I believe that time on earth is one of the most precious gifts we have, and that we can all choose how we use it. I hope **The Little Book of Procrastination** *will inspire you to enjoy and make the most of every moment.*

THE LITTLE BOOK OF
PROCRASTINATION

Do you put things off?
Do you often think -
"I'll do that tomorrow" -
even when The Thing you
need or want to do is
quite simple and straightforward?

Nearly everyone puts things off.
It's a habit called procrastination
and it can make you and other
people feel frustrated,
confused, fed-up and tired out.
So why do we do it?

Procrastination is a uniquely
human activity.
You won't find cats and dogs doing it.

So somewhere during our evolution,
our species must have developed
procrastination as one way to cope
with an increasingly complex world.
And sometimes, it can,
in the short-term, reduce stress.
But usually, putting things off
causes more problems than it
solves.......

What kind of things do people
put off?

ANYTHING

You really can procrastinate about
anything
(and some of us do).

For example, you could put off: going to the doctor, opening bills, putting up a smoke alarm, replying to invitations, tidying up cupboards, writing your will, finishing DIY, getting fit, giving up smoking, finding a good job, learning a language, being creative, saying sorry, ending a relationship, starting one, spending time with friends, playing with your children, visiting your gran, having a baby...

6

.......or saying
"I love you"

Whatever you've been
putting off, the first step in
doing anything,
however big or small,
is to take a **deep breath**.

And then another ....

(and then one more,
just for luck).

Why do we put things off?
When we know that it's usually much
better to do The Thing today
rather than tomorrow?

There are more reasons why
we put things off
than it's worth imagining.
Each reason is better than the last.
Each one causes us stress and
steals away our time, energy,
and enjoyment of life.
It's no surprise that procrastination is
known as the 'thief of time'.

And if there are many reasons for
putting things off,
there is also no one, magical,
universal solution to the problem
of procrastination.

*(Because if people could "just do it",
they would)*

But if there were one solution,
it would probably be
love.

When you love yourself,
you value your time
and the unique gifts
you can contribute to the world

When you love and respect
other people,
you want to give them the best
of all that you are,
and all that you have.

And when you love life,
you know that
every moment
and every gift
is too precious to be wasted.

But sometimes we forget
what we love
and we forget that
life is short -

- and then we procrastinate.

We all have the capacity to be
relaxed and productive,
and to do what we need to do with
energy and excitement.
We've all faced difficulties and
overcome them, and we've all
had experiences which have taught
us about life and how to live it.

We can draw on these strengths
when it comes to procrastination.
So even if you keep putting things off,
you're feeling **REALLY STUCK**,
and you can't imagine where to begin,
you **do** have the ability to get going
and get the job done.

Remember to be gentle with yourself.
Habits take time to develop, and time
to change. Putting things off is
a habit which you can change
one step at a time.

Whatever you are putting off,
please don't label yourself
"a procrastinator".
Labels are for bottles and boxes,

not people.

If you must call yourself something,
be playful and affirming: try

the Fairy-Good-Enough

or

**The-Silly-Sod-Who-Gets-There-
in-the-End,** for example.

Definitely preferable to
"a procrastinator".

It's much better to think of yourself
as someone who puts things off
now and again, but who can be
INCREDIBLY DYNAMIC

(and surprisingly effective)
at other times.

22

Which naturally leads you to wonder –

"I wonder how easy or hard it will be for me this time?"

Then you can be curious and interested in what happens when you start doing The Thing, rather than pessimistic and hopeless.

Imagine what life will be like when
The Thing you've been postponing
is behind you.
What will you do next?
How will you
REWARD yourself ?

What reward would really **motivate**
you and help you stay committed
to The Thing you have to do?
A glass of wine? A massage?
Game of tennis? A walk in the park?
A quiet read? Time with friends?
A long hot bath? A hug? A big bonus?
A fabulous holiday? Peace of mind?

You know. You choose.

26

99% of the time,
there is someone somewhere
who can and will help you
overcome whatever problem you
have with The Thing you are putting
off, no matter how large,
small or difficult it is.

The trick is to find that person….

.... and then to ask
for their help.

Asking for help or advice doesn't make you daft, weak, soft, needy, dependent or stupid.

It makes you human.

And people often enjoy being asked.

Make a list of everyone you know
who might be willing to become
your ally in dealing with
The Thing you are putting off.

Picture yourself getting great advice
and following it through.
Picture yourself working together with
your allies, and getting the job done.
Picture how you will feel as you relax
together afterwards.
Now, pick up the phone….

However, if you notice that you keep
procrastinating despite all the help
and advice you've received,
then something else is happening.

Maybe you're asking the
wrong questions?
Or maybe you don't like
what you hear?

Perhaps the truth is that you just
really don't want to do The Thing
you keep putting off.
Saying **"no"** can sometimes
be very difficult.
But it may be the most honest, helpful
thing to say in the circumstances.
Once you say it, you and everyone
else involved has the opportunity to
find other possibilities.

Saying a straightforward **"no"**
to the tasks, roles and responsibilities
you don't want to take on declutters
your life, frees your energy and
enables you to get on with what
you **do** want to do with more
enthusiasm, clarity and commitment.
And it puts you in a better position to
negotiate with other people about the
things they don't want to do either.

34

On the other hand, perhaps you really
DO want to do The Thing
(and you may even know that you'll
enjoy it once you get going),
but your imagination keeps producing
WORRIES and **DOUBTS**.

What if...?
What if...?
What if...?

When you know what you want to do (even if you think it's going to be tough), the only way forward is to **STOP** asking and **STOP** imagining and **STOP** worrying about possible outcomes, and get started with the first, practical step towards your goal.

When you do something in the real
world (*even a small something*), and
not just in your imagination,
you will get

EXPERIENCE, FEEDBACK and INFORMATION.

This will help you decide
what to do next.

Break down The Thing you have
to do into steps.
How long will the first step take?
(even a tiny one)
When could you make time for that?

(maybe ....today?)

And then after the first step, comes
the next and the next and the next
and the next and the next and the next
and the next and the next and the next ....
And look what's happened -
YOU'VE DONE IT!!

YES!

It's easy to forget that even the most boring or difficult task will eventually come to an end. When you know how long The Thing you're putting off will take, you can start to imagine what life will be like afterwards.

THINK ABOUT THE TIME
THINGS TAKE.

How long do you think
The Thing you are putting
off will take?

5 minutes, half an hour,
all day, 3 weeks, 6 months?

Picture yourself doing what you
need to do.

Picture yourself finishing it, effortlessly.

Picture yourself afterwards,
full of relief and relaxation.

Ask everyone who believes in you to write **"*You can do it!*"** on a piece of paper. Make a collage of all the messages and stick it somewhere noticeable. Look at it every time you feel like putting off what you are trying to accomplish.

You can do it! You can do it!

You can do it! You can do it!

You can do it! You can do it!

43

Friends listen to your fears and
fantasies about The Thing
you are putting off. But they still
encourage you to give it a go.
They encourage you to stick with it,
point out when you're being
perfectionist, celebrate with you
when the job's done.
What more could you ask?

So if a really good friend
promised you that
he or she would help you,
and then broke that promise,
how would you feel?
And if they did it again?
And again?

Every time you say to yourself,
"I'll do that Thing tomorrow",
and then when the next day comes,
you don't do it,
you are basically breaking a
promise to yourself.

Trusting ourselves plays a big part in
being self-confident, happy and creative.
If you break your own promises,
you feel guilty, negative, and
your self-esteem plummets.
Re-building trust in your ability
to follow your plans and decisions,
brings hope.

Be your own Best Friend.

Only make promises to yourself
that you know you'll keep.

Smile at The Thing you've been
avoiding. Say to yourself,
**"And now for the next
challenge!"**
Smiling releases
feel-good hormones.
Guaranteed to make you feel better
whatever you have to do.

In other words,
RELAX!

If you grit your teeth to force yourself to do The Thing you've been putting off, you'll restrict the blood flow in your face and throat, which will make you feel even more tense.

If you deliberately increase the
amount you move physically,
you won't procrastinate as much.
Our physical, mental, emotional
and spiritual systems and selves are
not separate, so increasing your
strength and fitness will enable you to
face even daunting challenges with
fresh self-confidence.

This doesn't mean you have to go to the gym five times a week, unless you want to. But it can mean taking the stairs rather than the lift, walking rather than using the car, running and stretching and bending and dancing and jumping and skipping and climbing and hopping, whether you need to or not.

Moving your body more means
enjoying being alive in every
cell of your body.
Imagine your body as the channel
through which you can follow
the river of your ideas, beliefs, dreams
and desires, and turn them into
reality through **ACTION**.

Fast walking in the fresh air,
swinging your arms,
looking around and taking deep
breaths, all stir your energies,
lift your spirit
and make you feel full of bounce
and determination.

(Putting things off doesn't)

Right now, give your face,
shoulders, arms, lower back and thighs
a quick rub. Stamp on the ground a
few times. Wave your hands vigorously
from the wrist, give yourself a shake
like a wet dog and
GROAN LOUDLY THREE TIMES.
Then blow yourself a big kiss
(or two) in the mirror.

56

Feel more energized?
Think you could tackle The Thing
you've been putting off?
Great.
Go for it.

(If not, repeat three times a day
until you're ready).

Or try putting on some

REALLY LOUD MUSIC

And get The Thing you're avoiding
done in half the time.

Everything we do, we do in stages.
You can move through each stage
effortlessly and happily.
Or you can procrastinate, get stuck,
feel bad, and lose your way.
You can start to **get unstuck** by
understanding where you get blocked.

The Action Spiral

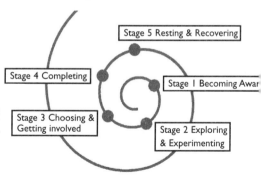

Stage 5 Resting & Recovering

Stage 4 Completing

Stage 1 Becoming Awar

Stage 3 Choosing &
Getting involved

Stage 2 Exploring
& Experimenting

The first stage of any activity is
BECOMING AWARE
of what you need or want to do.

Sometimes it's obvious.
Sometimes other people have to
point things out to us.
And sometimes we know, but we
manage to "forget".

If you block awareness, you may put
off things that affect your physical,
mental, emotional or financial health
(like taking care of your body,
dealing with stress, confronting difficult
emotional issues, paying bills,
making love or even having fun).

You might also "forget" promises
or commitments.
It's not that you're being deliberately
thoughtless or unkind. It's just that
you're not recognizing the importance
of The Thing (to you or other
people), or making it a priority.
And the consequence can be that
you – or I – can become neglectful.

Spend a few moments today on
your own, in a peaceful place,
and breathe slowly.

Think about what matters to you.
What do you need to do about it?

And what matters to the
people you care about?

What could you do about this?

To help yourself stay aware of
The Things you need to do, post
brightly coloured notes in places you
can't miss – the bathroom mirror, on
the kettle, on the back of the front
door. Leave messages on your own
mobile or answering machine.
You could even ask your nearest and
dearest to remind you
(*if you are feeling very bold*).

Raise your general level of awareness
by spending time each day paying
attention to your senses.
Listen to the sounds around you.

How have they changed
since yesterday?

Sit in a park and notice the different
ways in which people, animals
and trees move.
Allow yourself to savour tastes,
smells and textures.
Drink it all in.

Tune in to your body, and notice if
you are feeling any tension.
Have a word with your muscles.
Tell them it's OK to relax,
and then enjoy a good yawn
and a stretch.

Sometimes people put off doing things they would actually enjoy. It can seem hard to prioritise having fun, pleasure, relaxation, or even to find the kind of creative work you'd love to get lost in. These good feelings and experiences aren't really options.

They are NECESSITIES.

Without them, your spirit is crushed.
Procrastination is the kind of habit
that grows when

JOY, FUN AND PLEASURE
are in short supply.

72

How many of the things you really,
really love to do in life do you make
time for on a weekly basis?
Could you double that number?
Treble it?
What would life be like if you did?

You deserve to feel that good.

Anti-Procrastination Prescription:

LAUGHTER

is good for you

So share five large doses daily
(*minimum*).

The second stage of any activity is
EXPLORING and
EXPERIMENTING
with all the possible ways
of doing what you need or
want to do.

This could involve — thinking, imagining, talking, researching, planning. You can put off doing any of these things, perhaps because you feel overwhelmed by the task, because even thinking about it brings you out in a cold sweat, or because you feel so stuck you can't come up with any ways to move forward.

Remember that **thinking about doing** The Thing is probably very different from **actually doing it**.

Find a **ROLE-MODEL**, someone you think of as calm, creative and clear thinking, and just for a while, pretend you have all their skills, abilities and qualities.

ROLE-MODELS come in many shapes and sizes. It could be -

- Someone you know or have known
- A famous person, dead or alive
- Fantasy characters, from myths & legends
- A part of yourself

Choose someone whose capabilities you admire, and approach The Thing from a new perspective.

Imagine this person as your personal coach or trainer – picture the two of you together in discussion. Where would you be? What would he or she say to you, as you begin to plan your first step? What ideas would he or she come up with? What support could your role-model offer you?

For other people, generating ideas and talking about big plans is not a problem. In fact, they enjoy it so much they find it hard to move on to making their dreams a reality.
Give yourself permission to learn from and enjoy the journey as much as the dream, and the freedom to make the most of whatever happens.

At the third stage, you have to
CHOOSE the way forward,
and **GET INVOLVED**
in each step of
your decision.

If this stage is a problem for you,
you probably buy one more
de-cluttering book before you start
throwing anything away: read one
more diet before you start trying to
lose weight: ask one more person
before deciding where to go on
holiday... or you make a choice,
and then quickly reverse it.
Back to Square 1.

Ignore the little voice that whispers,
"You don't know enough".
Taking the first real-world step will
teach you the most.

Choosing can be challenging.
Some choices are enormous.
Where to live? Who to share our
lives with? What career to become
immersed in? What to believe in?
What causes to support?
Taking time to make major decisions
like these isn't procrastination
– it's good sense.

But taking time can turn
into procrastination,
if we keep trying to find a way
to have it all.

Because every choice we make
involves loss as well as gain,
which can be hard.

Perhaps we lose most
by putting off making the choice.
Because then what we lose is time —
and life is short.

Our options may disappear,
and if we don't choose,
life may make the choice for us.

But once you've made your decision -
your energy is released!
You are freed from the to-ing
and fro-ing, the if-ing and but-ing, and
you can finally step out into the light
and get going.

*All you have to do
now is keep going.*

Staying involved in what you have
decided to do
can take tenacity, courage and
determination.
(A sense of humour also helps)

Do you remember anyone from your childhood who was good at staying involved?
How did he or she do that?
Could you borrow some of that energy?

Never under-estimate the power of
ROUTINE.

Showing up at the same task at the
same time each day or each week
with an open mind
and a willing heart
will get the job done.

And over time, you'll find you're no longer relying on sheer will-power. What started out as hard work might even become enjoyable, and you may be surprised by sudden, unexpected

BURSTS of ENERGY.

If you have a hugely untidy desk,
cupboard, drawer, kitchen,
garden shed, LIFE (!) −
then start small. Put absolutely
everything from one corner into a
cardboard box, and keep
that place totally clear for a week.
Keep looking at that empty space −
how does it make you feel?

94

Now try increasing the size of
the cleared corner.
DE-CLUTTERING is an activity that
generates its own energy.
Once you get started, you might
find that you feel so much better,
you don't really want to stop.

The power of plodding. . .
if you de-cluttered your home by just
one thing each day, by the end of the
year, you would have
moved a mountain.

Two things a day? Two mountains!
Sometimes the tortoise really does
get there faster than the hare...

If you've been putting off paperwork
because you don't enjoy being alone
to do it, surround yourself with
pictures of your friends, or have
photographs of your family made
into a mouse-mat.

If you long to write,
but keep putting it off,
you can find the time somewhere.
Once you find it, guard it fiercely.
Cultivate a hatred of waste.

Some people procrastinate about writing because they don't know how to start. The trick is, you don't have to start at the beginning. Start anywhere you like, and work backwards and forwards until you know what you want to say back at the beginning. Then say it.

MAGIC!

People also procrastinate about writing – and reading – because they were not taught properly in the first place. There is absolutely no shame in finding help, support and good teaching now – you deserve it.

To keep yourself on track
with your tasks and objectives,
LIST-MAKING can be
extremely helpful, so long as –

- you don't do all the easy things and keep avoiding the hard ones
- you don't use making the list as a way to put off what you should be doing
- you can find the list

If you like lists, make them work even
better by creating different sections
using different coloured pens
(to do, to phone, to e-mail, to buy,
to clear up, etc.).
Tick off each item as you do it,
or give yourself a gold star.
Share your list with a friend and
compare (or contrast) progress.

Sometimes the same old things keep
mysteriously turning up on list after
list, and they never get done.
Try writing one of these in the middle
of a piece of paper.
What is the first step?
Write this down on another piece of
paper, and **make it your absolute
priority for the day**.

Start on this priority
before anything else.
Even if it is the beginning of an
enormous task, or a life-goal,
you will have made some progress.

Alternatively, you could forget making lists of what you **should** do, and keep a list, as you go, of what you **have done.** This becomes a
DIARY of SUCCESS.
Try this for a couple of weeks, and notice not only how much you actually do, but how you are getting more and more effective each day.

A MINI-REWARD can keep you
going, even if it is something as simple
as ten minutes dreaming
in the sunshine....

*What have you done today,
to make you feel proud?*

YES!

The fourth stage of action is
COMPLETION.

The End

Sometimes we put off completing
because we fear

FAILURE,

worrying that what we've done
isn't good enough.

Alternatively, we
might fear success.
Maybe we'll really
make it this time –

THEN WHAT ????

Or we may simple be worried
about completing
because we don't know
what will happen next.
The future looks a bit empty,
without that old
familiar Thing hanging over us.

So we also procrastinate about
leaving jobs, values, people
and places which are not
really right for us anymore.

Remind yourself that whatever
happens, when you let go,
you can learn from it.

It's unlikely to be
the end of the world.
(And if it is, you can learn from that)

After a while, life will open up again,
with new possibilities
and new challenges.
You just need to know when to say
"enough", and how to complete.

Practice setting **TIME-LIMITS**
around what you want to do.
Imagine yourself in ten years time,
looking back. How much more time
would you recommend you spend
on this particular Thing?
How will you know when you've
done or said or tried enough?

DEADLINES

can be useful if they make you feel
full of energy and determination and
Let's Go For It!

(or maybe just help you get
the job done).

Deadlines are **not** helpful if they
make you moody, grumpy, miserable,
smoke, drink, binge,
shout at your family, kick the cat,
or vent your frustration on the
next driver to cut you up at the lights
(even if they deserve it).

Only agree deadlines
with people you respect

(Think about it)

Deadlines can help you
recognise that
enough
is
ENOUGH.

And it usually is.

And if you really have finished,
achieved your goals and
fulfilled your dreams –

CONGRATULATIONS!

It's time to celebrate and
savour the sweet taste of success.

Don't put off having a party!!!

Of course some endings and
completions aren't celebratory.
They may be painful, or sad.
Don't put off finding the support
you need. Another time, it will be
you offering the shoulder,
the listening ear and the quietly
receptive heart.

However happy or sad the ending,
all the time you've been involved,
all the way to completion, you have
been developing your ability to trust
yourself, to be committed and
reliable. You've been building up a
deep memory bank of **doing what
you said you'd do** – and
that is a treasure you can never lose.

It can sometimes be hard to find the
energy to complete.
If this is true for you
at the moment, don't be hard
on yourself.

Maybe you've been stressed for a long time and you're a bit run down.

Procrastination may simply be a signal from your system that you need to withdraw for a while, and get some (well-earned) rest.

If someone who is usually productive
and effective starts procrastinating a lot,
or can only get enthused by new
projects but can't complete, they might
be suffering from serious difficulties,
like **BURN-OUT, DEPRESSION**
or **A PHYSICAL PROBLEM**.
These symptoms need to be checked
out – see a doctor, and get some help.

The final stage of any activity,
after completion, is to
REST and RECOVER.

Can you remember the last time you woke up feeling **really refreshed**? No?

People put off pausing as much as they put off taking action, even though we all know we need breaks.

If this is you, **stop right now!**

It can be tempting to rush on after
you have reached completion.
Allowing yourself to **PAUSE**
before you do so will give you space
to become aware of and to reflect on
what you have learned.
Then you will be clearer about
your next direction.

Take a breath, let out a big sigh and relax your shoulders.
Close your eyes, and let yourself imagine lying on a beautiful, warm, sandy beach. Listen to the waves quietly breaking on the sand, and feel the hot sun gently kissing your face…..

Some people worry that if they stop,
they will never get started again. This
is highly unlikely – but it's probably a
reflection of how tired they have
allowed themselves to get.
Take regular pauses, at the end of
mini-spirals of activity, and notice
how your energy rises.

Allowing ourselves to pause means
saying **_"no"_**
to more involvement, for the moment,
and being
OPEN TO THE
UNPREDICTABLE.

This may feel unfamiliar,
or even scary at first.
But once you get used to it, you will
find you cherish those moments
of stillness and calm in
which insights appear, and
love, intimacy and spontaneity
have space to grow.

When you can
**really rest deeply, you
can really, really exert yourself**.
And that is when you know your habit
of procrastination is finally
making an exit. It might come back
at times of stress,
but it won't stay long.

Procrastination doesn't happen
in a vacuum, although it can be
a very isolating habit.

As you continue to use your time and
energy more productively, you may
start to notice the way other people
around you handle theirs.

If your partner procrastinates, it can be irritating, frustrating or worse. What do you do?

Ignore them? Nag ? Shout? Sulk?
Make threats?
Offer bribes (chocolate, sex,
a night out with the lads/girls)?
Or do you do The Thing yourself ?
(with the air of a wounded
martyr, naturally)

Most of us resort to this kind of thing,
when our nearest and dearest
are driving us up the wall
by putting off doing little
(or even middle-sized or
enormous) things.

And sometimes, it has to be said,
these low-down tactics work.

But for a truly lasting effect, like developing a great relationship, it's probably better to find a more straightforward approach.

Such as taking care of yourself, getting rid of your own bad habits, and negotiating in clear, loving, and respectful ways.

When children procrastinate
(over homework, tidying rooms,
relaying information, making dates
with friends, etc.) it can also be
frustrating and/or worrying.
Mostly, it's just a part of growing up
and experimenting with activity
and passivity, cause and effect,
control and power.

143

Openly dealing with your own
procrastination, and letting the
benefits speak for themselves,
will go a long way.
The time to be concerned is if your
child's procrastination becomes
habitual, problematic or dangerous.

Talk directly to your son or daughter about what might help, and what might motivate them.

Find support from friends, teachers or a counsellor.

You probably want the children
in your life to have role-models
who can show them
how not to procrastinate.

What would such a person be like?

Someone who doesn't deny difficulties, but who faces responsibility; who takes a deep breath and moves forward. Someone who is fully, joyfully alive, exploring, initiating, open to possibilities and to sharing the journey through to completion, and rest.

Someone like you.

*If you used to procrastinate a lot,
the world may have lost
some of its fresh beauty.
Everything would have begun to
look the same, as you woke each day
with the same old Thing looming
over you, and the same old heavy,
guilty feelings.*

*So I hope that somewhere in these
pages, you have found something that
strikes a chord, rings a bell,
or gives you hope.
Many other people have struggled to
overcome procrastination, and won.
You can too. I wish you happiness and
excitement, love and generosity,
every step of the way.*

ALSO BY ANDREA PERRY

Isn't It About Time?
How to stop putting things off and get on with your life Worth Publishing, 2002
ISBN 1903269032   288 pages   £8.99
Available from all good bookshops or from
Worth Publishing (www.worthpublishing.com)

Comments on "Isn't It About Time?"

"I was totally impressed with it. It's rare that I come across a self-help book that I actually enjoy... this is very helpful." Dr. Pam Spurr, Psychologist (LBCRadio)

"It made me think, laugh and get on with this review."
Dr. Geoff Pelham, CPJ Review

"This book should come with a written warning. You no longer have any excuses. It makes you horribly productive" Susan Elderkin, novelist, Granta List 2003

Andrea Perry is a dramatherapist, psychotherapist and writer, who works with individuals and groups in therapy, the NHS, in higher education and the business world.

For more information on Andrea Perry's **PROCRASTINATION WORKSHOPS**, please contact Worth Publishing. (www.worthpublishing.com)